THAT'S MY JAM!

# POP MUSIC

BY NATHAN SOMMER

EUREKA!, AN IMPRINT OF BELLWETHER MEDIA BY FLUTTERBEE

eureka!

***Eureka!*** books turn real stories into unforgettable experiences. Clear, direct language and sharp, captivating imagery make it easy to follow your curiosity, one fascinating fact at a time.
Your Eureka! moment awaits!

This edition first published in 2027 by Bellwether Media, Inc.



For information regarding permission, write to Bellwether Media, Inc., Attention: Permissions Department, 3500 American Blvd W, Suite 150, Bloomington, MN 55431.

Library of Congress Cataloging-in-Publication Data

Names: Sommer, Nathan author
Title: Pop music / by Nathan Sommer.
Description: Eureka. | Minneapolis : Bellwether Media, Inc, 2027. | Series: That's my jam! | Includes index. | Audience: Ages 9-13 | Audience: Grades 7-9 | Summary: ""Engaging images accompany information on pop music. The text level and subject matter are intended for students in grades 5 through 9"-Provided by publisher"-- Provided by publisher.
Identifiers: LCCN 2026001556 (print) | LCCN 2026001557 (ebook) | ISBN 9798898801267 (library binding) | ISBN 9798898802509 (ebook)
Subjects: LCSH: Popular music--History and criticism
Classification: LCC ML3470 .S614 2027 (print) | LCC ML3470 (ebook) | DDC 782.42164--dc23/eng/20260128

LC record available at https://lccn.loc.gov/2026001556
LC ebook record available at https://lccn.loc.gov/2026001557

Editor: Elizabeth Neuenfeldt Series Designer: Josh Brink

Printed in the United States of America, North Mankato, MN.

# TABLE OF CONTENTS

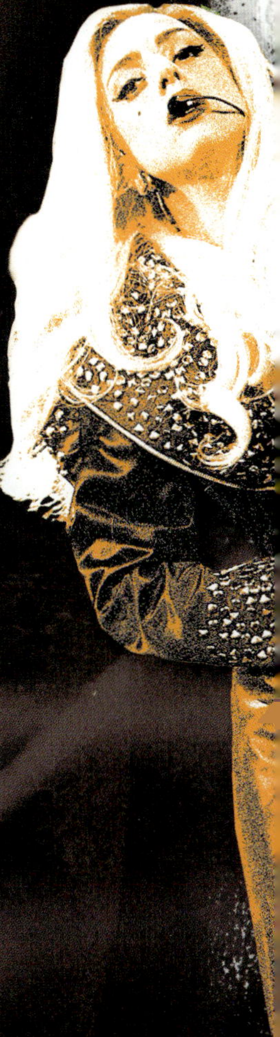

# WHAT IS POP?

Pop music comes from the word "popular." This wide-ranging genre features catchy melodies and upbeat music. It has grown to include elements of hip-hop, R & B, and country. Pop songs appeal to mainstream audiences. Many cover relatable subjects such as love, friendship, and celebration.

TAYLOR SWIFT

## BEHIND THE SONG

**Pop songs usually include two to three verses. Choruses follow the verses. Verses use different words to tell a song's story. Choruses repeat memorable phrases that are the song's main message.**

ARIANA GRANDE

Dance-pop and pop rock are well-known types of pop. Latin pop and K-pop are also popular subgenres. Taylor Swift, Ariana Grande, and BTS are some of pop's biggest artists today.

BTS

# THE HISTORY OF POP

Popular music has been around for a long time. Many believe today's modern pop began in the 1950s. The *Billboard* Hot 100 chart was created in 1958. This chart ranks songs by their sales and airplay. It helps determine the world's most popular songs.

ELVIS PRESLEY

Billboard HOT 100

## THE FIRST #1 HIT

The first *Billboard* Hot 100 chart came out on August 4, 1958. "Poor Little Fool" by Ricky Nelson was its first number one hit. More than 1,100 songs have topped the chart since then.

Rock and roll often inspired early pop. Synthesizers were popular by the 1970s. Funk and disco soon followed.

MICHAEL JACKSON

MTV changed pop music forever in 1981. This TV channel aired music videos. People could now watch their favorite songs. The channel favored bold artists with stylish looks. Michael Jackson and Madonna became superstars.

## STREAMING POP MUSIC

**Streaming platforms such as Spotify allow listeners to play any song at any time. Spotify's streams became a part of the *Billboard* Hot 100 chart in 2012.**

Pop stars of the 1990s and 2000s collaborated with hip-hop and R & B artists. Today, social media platforms such as TikTok and YouTube influence pop music. They help lesser-known artists create viral hits.

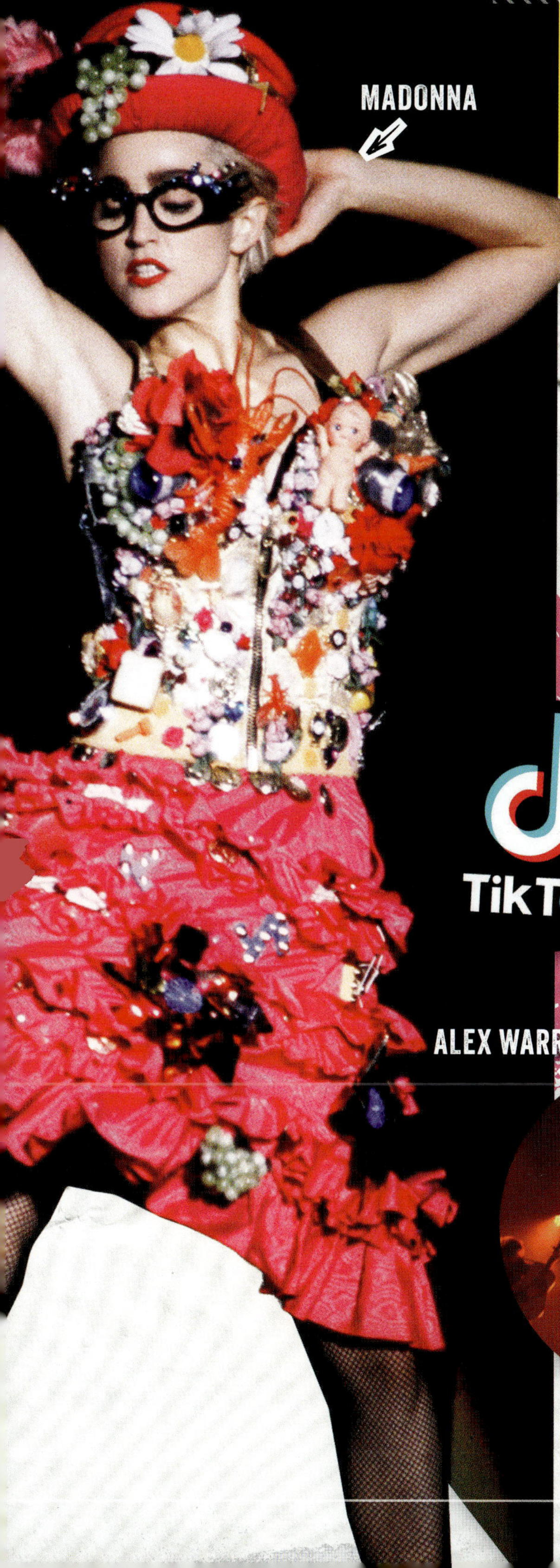

MADONNA

JAY-Z AND BEYONCÉ

ALEX WARREN

# POP TIMELINE

## 1958

The first *Billboard* Hot 100 chart is created to recognize music's most popular songs

## 1981

MTV goes live, quickly popularizing music videos

## 1967

"Star Collector" by the Monkees becomes one of the first pop songs to use a synthesizer, an instrument that soon defines the genre

## 1983

Madonna releases her first album and later becomes the best-selling female pop artist of all time

## 1982

Michael Jackson's *Thriller* album is released, eventually becoming the best-selling pop album of all time

## 2005

**YouTube launches, making pop music videos available to their widest audience yet**

BOBBY BROWN

## 1990

**"She Ain't Worth It" by Glenn Medeiros featuring Bobby Brown becomes the first pop and hip-hop collaboration to top the *Billboard* Hot 100**

## 2007

**Digital streams become a part of the *Billboard* Hot 100 list**

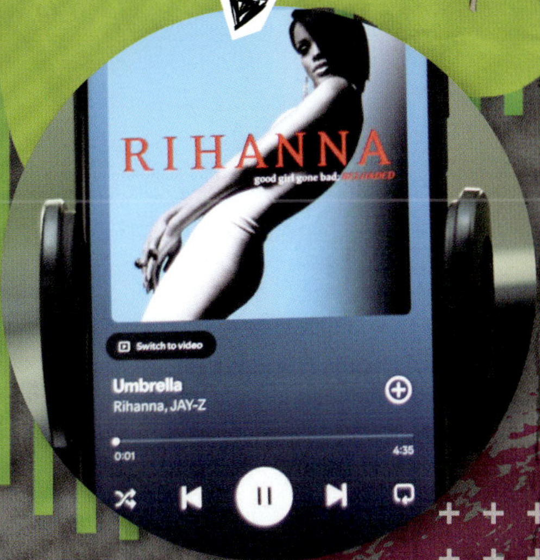


## 2016

**TikTok is released, allowing a new generation of artists to achieve viral pop success**

LOREN GRAY

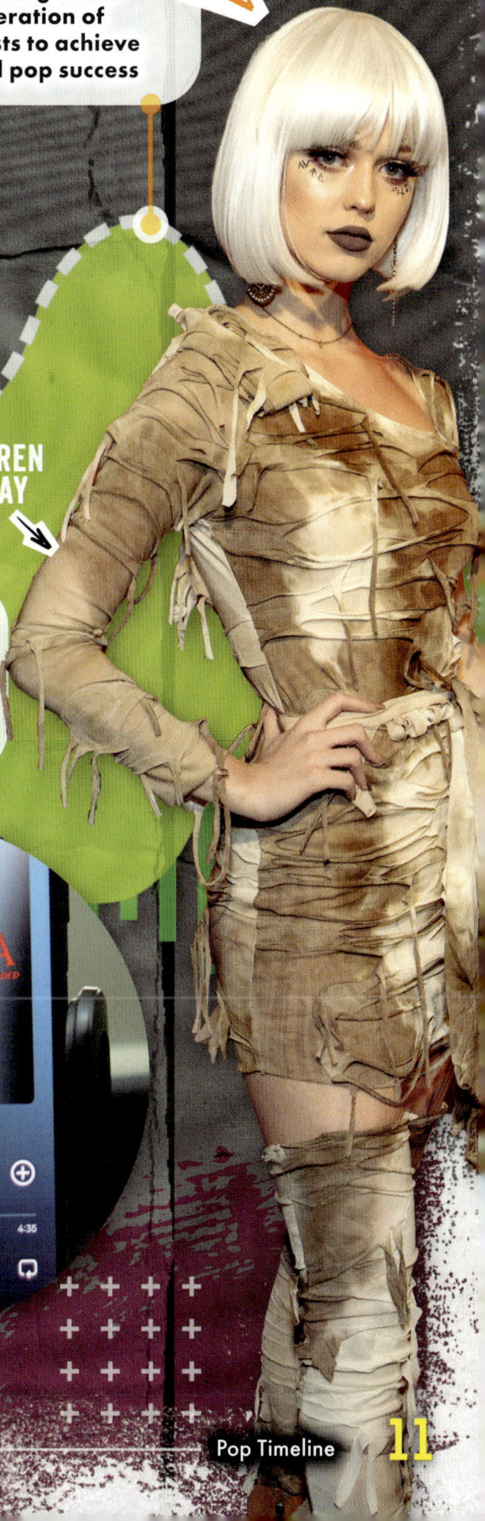

# INSTRUMENTS

## SYNTHESIZER

Robert Moog invented the modern synthesizer in 1964. It allows musicians to create many sounds digitally. Pop rock artists such as the Beatles made synthesizers popular.

## THE INVENTOR OF AUTO-TUNE

**Dr. Andy Hildebrand invented Auto-Tune in 1997. His idea came from the wife of a friend. She joked about a device that could help them sing.**

## DIGITAL AUDIO WORKSTATIONS (DAWS)

Modern pop music is mostly produced using computers. DAWs record high-quality vocals and mix them with beats made on the same device. The first DAW was called the Soundstream. It hit shelves in 1977.

CHER

## AUTO-TUNE

Auto-Tune edits and corrects an artist's vocals. This helps create perfect melodies. "Believe" by Cher came out in 1998. It was the first major song to use this technology.

# AWARDS AND HONORS

## GRAMMY AWARDS

The Grammys have been music's highest honor since 1959. Pop awards include Best Dance Pop Recording and Best Pop Vocal Album. Winners are decided by votes from other musicians and producers.

## MTV VIDEO VANGUARD AWARD

**The MTV Video Vanguard Award is the VMAs' lifetime accomplishment award. It honors artists who have left a lasting mark on music videos. Past winners include Britney Spears and Shakira.**

JANET JACKSON

## *BILLBOARD* MUSIC AWARDS

The first *Billboard* Music Awards were held in 1990. These recognize the year's most-played songs and best-selling albums. Winners are based on sales and airplay.

## MTV VIDEO MUSIC AWARDS (VMAS)

The VMAs began in 1984. The event honors popular music videos each year. It also allows pop's superstars to perform their hits. Top awards include Video of the Year and Best Pop Artist.

CYNDI LAUPER

# TYPES OF POP

## POP ROCK

**Date Started:** 1950s

**Traits:**
- upbeat music
- features guitars and drums

**Song:** "I'm Still Standing" by Elton John

## COUNTRY POP

**Date Started:** 1960s

**Traits:**
- mixes acoustic guitars with digital beats
- upbeat pace
- heartfelt and relatable songwriting

**Song:** "High Horse" by Kacey Musgraves

THE ARCHIES

KAROL G

## BUBBLEGUM POP

**Date Started:** 1960s

**Traits:**

- catchy, simple melodies
- memorable, lighthearted lyrics
- often appeals to younger fans

**Song:**

"Sugar, Sugar" by the Archies

## LATIN POP

**Date Started:** 1960s

**Traits:**

- strong rhythms
- blends Latin instruments with current pop sounds
- emotional and cultural storytelling

**Song:**

"Si Antes Te Hubiera Conocido" by Karol G

# K-POP

**Date Started:** 1990s

**Traits:**

- mixes pop and hip-hop with Korean instruments
- catchy choruses and melodies
- high-energy choreography

**Song:**

"Boy With Luv" by BTS and Halsey

# DANCE-POP

**Date Started:** 1980s

**Traits:**

- dance-floor-ready beats
- synth-heavy electronic production
- often includes empowering messages

**Song:**

"We Found Love" by Rihanna

## INDIE POP

**Date Started:** 1970s

**Traits:**
- quirky and experimental sound
- blends pop melodies with rock and punk influences
- heavy use of guitars and drums

**Song:** "Such Great Heights" by the Postal Service

## POP HIP-HOP

**Date Started:** 1980s

**Traits:**
- often a collaboration between artists from each genre
- combines pop with hip-hop rhythms
- mixture of sung vocals with rapped verses

**Song:** "Nothin' on You" B.o.B. featuring Bruno Mars

# POP PROFILES
## CHER

Cher is nicknamed the Goddess of Pop. She is a trailblazer in music and film.

### SONNY & CHER

Cher's career began with the duo Sonny & Cher. They starred in the 1970s TV show *The Sonny & Cher Comedy Hour.*

**Birthday:**
May 20, 1946

**Hometown:**
El Centro, California

**Types of Music:**
folk-pop, pop rock, dance-pop

**First Hit Song:**
"I Got You Babe" (1965)

## TIMELINE

**1965**
Achieves first *Billboard* number one hit with "I Got You Babe"

**1988**
Cher wins an Oscar for Best Actress in a Leading Role

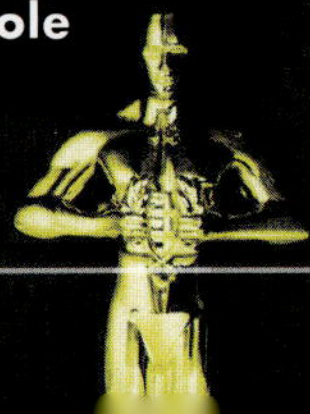

**2000**
"Believe" wins the Grammy for Best Dance Recording

## AUTO-TUNE ARTIST

Cher has sold over 100 million records. She has experimented with rock, dance-pop, and other genres. She was the first major artist to use Auto-Tune.

## DECADES OF HITS

Cher is the only solo artist to top *Billboard* charts in seven straight decades. She has won a Grammy, an Emmy, and an Oscar. She was inducted into the Rock & Roll Hall of Fame in 2024.

## FROM POP STAR TO MOVIE STAR

**Cher's acting career took off in the 1980s. Her famous movies include *Moonstruck* and *Mamma Mia! Here We Go Again.***

## HIT RELEASES

- ***All I Really Want to Do*** **(1965)**
- ***Cher*** **(1987)**
- ***Heart of Stone*** **(1989)**
- ***Believe*** **(1998)**
- ***Dancing Queen*** **(2018)**

**2023**
**Cher becomes the first solo artist to top a *Billboard* chart in seven straight decades**

**2024**
**Cher is inducted into the Rock & Roll Hall of Fame**

# ELTON JOHN

Elton John is a pop rock pioneer. He is a world-class songwriter and pianist.

## WHIZ KID

John's piano skills earned him scholarships at age 11. His early work was inspired by rock and R & B. "Your Song" became John's first major hit in 1970.

## LGBTQ+ ICON

John's music is famous for its high energy. He often blends piano and electric guitar with soulful vocals. John was one of the first major artists to come out as LGBTQ+. He has sold over 300 million records.

## TOP PERFORMER

John is known for colorful fashions and bold showmanship. His huge list of hits makes him one of music's greatest performers.

**Birthday:**
March 25, 1947

**Hometown:**
Pinner, Middlesex, England

**Types of Music:**
pop rock, R & B, soul

**First Hit Song:**
"Your Song" (1970)

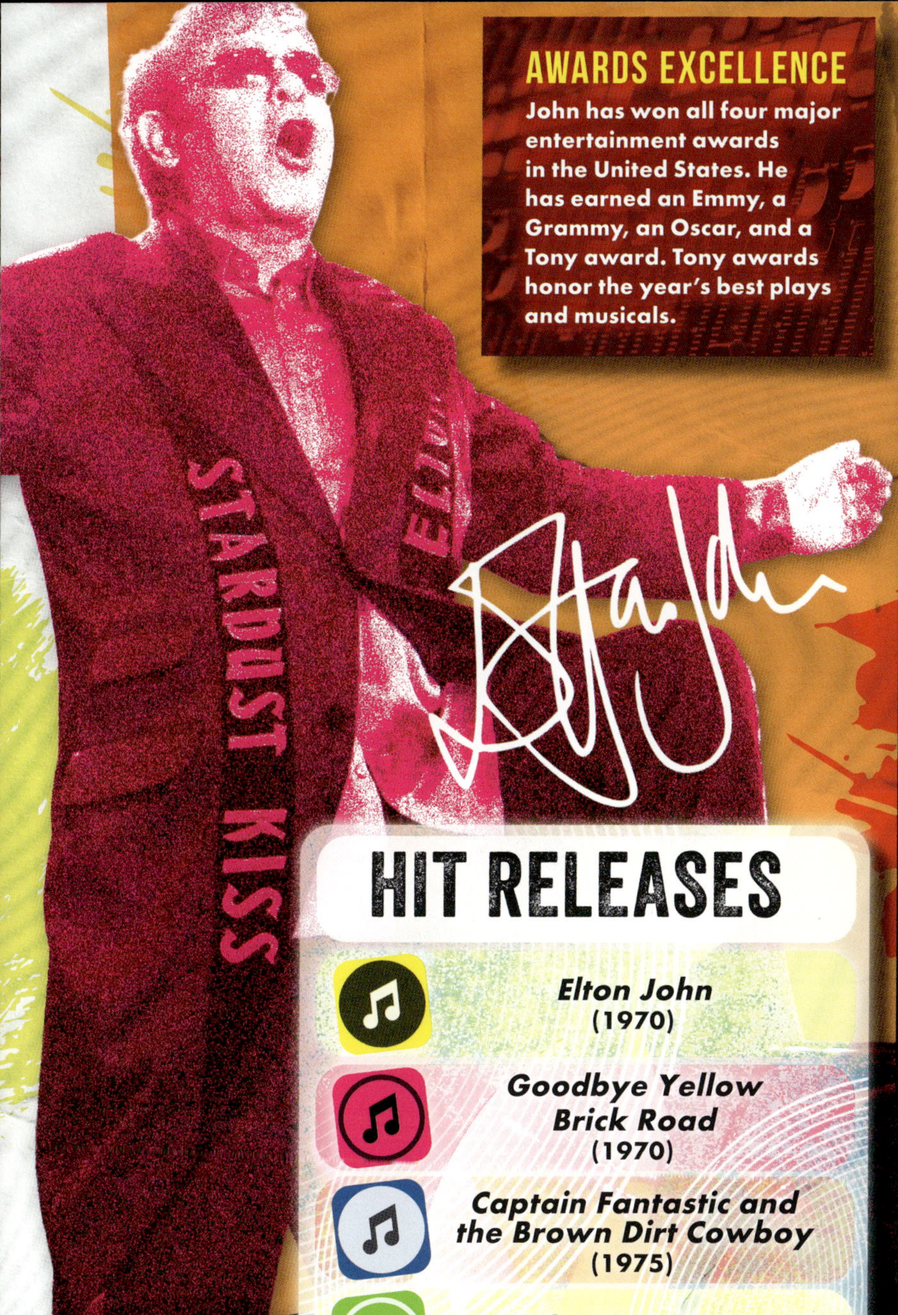


## AWARDS EXCELLENCE

John has won all four major entertainment awards in the United States. He has earned an Emmy, a Grammy, an Oscar, and a Tony award. Tony awards honor the year's best plays and musicals.

## HIT RELEASES

- *Elton John* (1970)
- *Goodbye Yellow Brick Road* (1970)
- *Captain Fantastic and the Brown Dirt Cowboy* (1975)
- *The Lion King* (1994)
- *Who Believes in Angels?* (2025)

## TIMELINE

**1958**
John is awarded a scholarship to the Royal Academy of Music in London

**1970**
"Your Song" becomes John's first major hit

**1973**
John earns his first of nine *Billboard* number one songs with "Crocodile Rock"

**1976**
John comes out as LGBTQ+

**1998**
John is knighted by Queen Elizabeth for his contributions to music and charity

# MICHAEL JACKSON

Michael Jackson is nicknamed the King of Pop. He was one of music's most influential artists.

## GOING SOLO

Jackson had huge success with the Jackson 5 during childhood. *Off the Wall* was his first solo album as an adult. It was a hit.

## BEST-SELLING ARTIST

Jackson's 1982 album *Thriller* is the best-selling album in history. It had seven songs chart in *Billboard*'s Top 10 list. It also won seven Grammys. Jackson was inducted into the Rock & Roll Hall of Fame twice.

## TIMELINE

**1964**
**The Jackson 5 debuts when Michael is five years old**

**1979**
**Jackson releases *Off the Wall*, his first solo album as an adult**

**1982**
**The *Thriller* album is released, eventually becoming the best-selling album of all time**

**Birthday:**
August 29, 1958

**Death:**
June 25, 2009

**Hometown:**
Gary, Indiana

**Types of Music:**
dance-pop, R & B, pop rock

**First Hit Song:**
"Ben" (1972)

## MUSIC VIDEO PIONEER

Jackson's career opened new doors for Black artists. Many believe he helped turn music videos into an art form.

## HIT RELEASES

***Ben***
(1972)

***Off the Wall***
(1979)

***Thriller***
(1982)

***Bad***
(1987)

***Dangerous***
(1991)

**2001**
Jackson is inducted into the Rock & Roll Hall of Fame as a solo artist

**2009**
Jackson passes away at age 50

# PRINCE

Many consider Prince a musical genius. He often blended soul and funk with pop.

## INSTRUMENT EXPERT

Prince's parents were jazz artists. He had mastered the piano, guitar, and drums by high school. Prince's first album came out in 1978. It was called *For You*. He played every instrument on the album.

## FROM MUSIC TO FILM

The *1999* album came out in 1982. It was a hit! He created the *Purple Rain* album and movie in 1984. The project earned him two Grammys and an Oscar.

**Birthday:**
August 29, 1958

**Death:**
April 21, 2016

**Hometown:**
Minneapolis, Minnesota

**Types of Music:**
soul, funk, R & B, pop rock

**First Hit Song:**
"I Wanna Be Your Lover" (1979)

## HIT RELEASES

*Prince* (1979)

*1999* (1982)

*Purple Rain* (1984)

*Around the World in a Day* (1985)

*Sign o' the Times* (1987)

### CHART DOMINATION

*Purple Rain* was a huge hit. It made Prince the first artist to have a number one film, song, and album at once.

### TIRELESS TALENT

Prince recorded nearly 40 albums. He wrote thousands of songs. His talent and thrilling performances changed pop's sound.

## TIMELINE

**1978**
Prince's debut album *For You* is released

**1982**
The *1999* album is released, becoming Prince's first worldwide success

**1984**
"When Doves Cry" from *Purple Rain* becomes Prince's first *Billboard* number one hit

**2004**
Prince is inducted into the Rock & Roll Hall of Fame

**2016**
Prince passes away at age 57

# MADONNA

Madonna is the best-selling female artist in history. Her groundbreaking career has helped define modern pop music.

## EARLY SUCCESS

Madonna studied dance in college. She performed in rock bands. Her first album, *Madonna*, came out in 1983. Its songs "Holiday" and "Borderline" were huge radio hits.

## HIT RELEASES

***Madonna*** **(1983)**

***Like a Prayer*** **(1989)**

***Ray of Light*** **(1998)**

***Music*** **(2000)**

***Confessions on a Dance Floor*** **(2005)**

## TIMELINE

**1983**
Madonna's debut album, *Madonna*, is released

**1988**
"Like a Prayer" is released, instantly becoming one of her most famous songs

**1999**
The *Ray of Light* album wins three Grammy awards

## EXPERIMENTAL ARTIST

Madonna has had 12 *Billboard* number one hits. She experiments with new looks and sounds on each album. Her 1998 album *Ray of Light* was a hit. It won the Grammy for Best Pop Album.

## POP TRAILBLAZER

Madonna has remained an icon. Her fearless attitude has inspired generations of female artists.

**Birthday:**
August 16, 1958

**Hometown:**
Bay City, Michigan

**Types of Music:**
dance-pop,
pop hip-hop, electronic

**First Hit Song:**
"Holiday" (1983)

**2009**
Madonna's Sticky & Sweet Tour becomes one of the best-selling tours in history

**2012**
Madonna headlines the Super Bowl Halftime Show

# BRITNEY SPEARS

Many call Britney Spears the Princess of Pop. She had countless hits throughout the late 1990s and 2000s.

## CHILD TV STAR

Spears starred in Disney's *The All-New Mickey Mouse Club* at age 11. Her 1999 debut *. . .Baby One More Time* made Spears a global superstar.

## HIT AFTER HIT

Spears's 2000 album *Oops!. . . I Did It Again* broke sales records. Her 2007 album *Blackout* is often called one of the greatest modern pop albums. "Hold It Against Me" came out in 2011. It became Spears's fifth *Billboard* number one song.

**Birthday:**
December 2, 1981

**Hometown:**
Kentwood, Louisiana

**Types of Music:**
bubblegum pop, dance-pop

**First Hit Song:**
". . .Baby One More Time" (1998)

## FAMOUS COSTARS

Spears is not the only superstar from *The All-New Mickey Mouse Club*. Her costars included Justin Timberlake and Christina Aguilera.

## GENERATIONAL TALENT

Spears has sold nearly 150 million records. Her music inspired a new generation of pop stars.

## HIT RELEASES

*. . .Baby One More Time* (1999)

*Oops!. . . I Did It Again* (2000)

*In the Zone* (2003)

*Blackout* (2007)

*Femme Fatale* (2011)

## TIMELINE

**1993**
Spears stars in Disney's *The All-New Mickey Mouse Club*

**1998**
". . .Baby One More Time" is released, hitting number one on the *Billboard* Hot 100

**2000**
The *Oops!. . . I Did It Again* album sells 1.3 million U.S. copies in one week

**2007**
The *Blackout* album is released, marking a huge comeback for Spears

**2011**
"Hold It Against Me" becomes Spears's fifth number one on the *Billboard* Hot 100

# SHAKIRA

Shakira is nicknamed the Queen of Latin Music. She is one of the best-selling Latin artists.

## HIT RELEASES

***MTV Unplugged***
**(2000)**

***Laundry Service***
**(2001)**

***She Wolf***
**(2009)**

***Shakira***
**(2014)**

***Las Mujeres Ya No Lloran***
**(2024)**

## TEEN SUPERSTAR

Shakira danced from a young age. She began writing music at age eight. At 14, she released her first album. Shakira's 2000 album *MTV Unplugged* earned a Grammy.

## TIMELINE

**1991**
**Shakira's debut album *Magia* is released**

**2001**
**Shakira's *MTV Unplugged* album wins the Grammy for Best Latin Pop Album**

**2006**
**"Hips Don't Lie" is released, topping charts around the world**

## WORLDWIDE CHART-TOPPER

Shakira's 2001 album *Laundry Service* sold more than 13 million copies. Her 2006 song "Hips Don't Lie" topped charts worldwide. It became one of the best-selling songs in history.

## A NEW AUDIENCE

Shakira has helped Latin pop reach global listeners. She has sold more than 80 million records.

**Birthday:**
February 2, 1977

**Hometown:**
Barranquilla, Colombia

**Types of Music:**
Latin pop, dance-pop, pop rock

**First Hit Song:**
"Ciega, Sordomuda" (1998)

**2010**
"Waka Waka (This Time for Africa)" is released, soon becoming one of the most-watched music videos in history

**2023**
Shakira wins the MTV Video Vanguard Award

# TAYLOR SWIFT

Taylor Swift is one of music's greatest storytellers. Her historic career has explored nearly every type of pop.

## TEEN COUNTRY STAR

Swift began songwriting and playing the guitar at age 12. Her early albums were country pop.

## MAKING HISTORY

Swift's 2014 album *1989* had three number one singles. In 2024, Swift became the first artist to win the Album of the Year Grammy four times. Later that year, her Eras Tour became history's best-selling concert.

**Birthday:**
December 13, 1989

**Hometown:**
West Reading, Pennsylvania

**Types of Music:**
country pop, folk pop, indie pop, dance-pop

**First Hit Song:**
"Tim McGraw" (2006)

## ● *BILLBOARD* ICON

As of 2026, Swift has had eight albums gain one million first-week sales. This is a music record. She has charted more than 275 songs on the *Billboard* Hot 100.

## HIT RELEASES

***Red*** **(2012)**

***1989*** **(2014)**

***Reputation*** **(2017)**

***Lover*** **(2019)**

***Midnights*** **(2022)**

## TIMELINE

**2006**
Swift's debut album, *Taylor Swift*, is released

**2010**
Swift's *Speak Now* album debuts with more than one million U.S. copies sold in its first week

**2012**
"We Are Never Ever Getting Back Together" becomes Swift's first number one single

**2014**
*1989* is released, earning three number one singles

**2024**
Swift becomes the first artist in history to win Album of the Year four times

# LADY GAGA

Lady Gaga is a one-of-a-kind talent. She has become a long-lasting icon.

## HIT RELEASES

***The Fame***
**(2008)**

***The Fame Monster***
**(2009)**

***Born This Way***
**(2011)**

***Chromatica***
**(2020)**

***Mayhem***
**(2025)**

### EARLY CHART-TOPPER

Lady Gaga learned piano at age four. Growing up, she looked up to David Bowie and the band Queen. Her first album *The Fame* came out in 2008. Two of its songs topped the *Billboard* Hot 100.

## TIMELINE

**2008**
**Gaga's debut album *The Fame* is released**

**2009**
**"Bad Romance" is released, soon becoming one of history's most-watched music videos**

**2011**
**The *Born This Way* album sells 1.1 million copies in its first week**

## OSCAR WINNER

Lady Gaga's 2009 "Bad Romance" became one of history's most-watched music videos. Her 2011 album *Born This Way* sold 1.1 million first-week copies. Her song "Shallow" earned an Oscar in 2019.

## FEARLESS PERFORMER

Lady Gaga has won 16 Grammys as of 2026. Her self-love and advocacy have helped millions of listeners find their voices.

## SONGWRITING SUPERSTAR

**Lady Gaga has also written music for artists including Britney Spears and Cher.**

**Birthday:**
**March 28, 1986**

**Hometown:**
**New York City, New York**

**Types of Music:**
**dance-pop, pop rock, jazz**

**First Hit Song:**
**"Just Dance" (2008)**

NEW YORK CITY

**2019**
**Gaga wins an Oscar for her song "Shallow" from the movie *A Star Is Born***

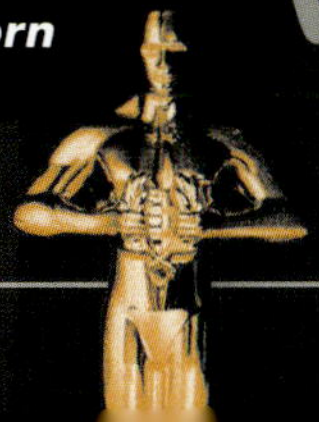

**2025**
**"Die With a Smile" becomes Gaga's sixth number one single**

# JUSTIN BIEBER

Justin Bieber went from teen pop star to music legend. He is one of the digital age's biggest artists.

## TEEN IDOL

Bieber played the drums and guitar growing up. He was discovered on YouTube. His first single "One Time" made him a global superstar at age 15.

## NUMEROUS NUMBER ONES

Bieber's 2010 song "Baby" was the first music video to get 500 million YouTube views. His 2015 album *Purpose* scored three chart-topping singles. Bieber's 2021 album *Justice* made him the youngest artist to have eight number one albums.

**Birthday:**
**March 1, 1994**

**Hometown:**
**Stratford, Canada**

**Types of Music:**
**bubblegum pop, dance-pop, R & B**

**First Hit Song:**
**"One Time" (2009)**

# HIT RELEASES

*My World* (2009)

*Believe* (2012)

*Purpose* (2015)

*Justice* (2021)

*SWAG* (2025)

## RECORD BREAKER

Bieber has sold around 150 million records. He holds many Guinness World Records.

# TIMELINE

**2007**
Bieber starts achieving viral success on YouTube

**2009**
Bieber's debut single "One Time" becomes a worldwide hit

**2010**
"Baby" is released, soon becoming the first music video with 500 million YouTube views

**2015**
The *Purpose* album includes three chart-topping songs

**2021**
Bieber becomes the youngest solo artist in history to have eight number one albums

# ARIANA GRANDE

Ariana Grande is one of music's most-streamed artists. She has ruled pop throughout the 2010s and 2020s.

## FINDING HER VOICE

Grande starred in Nickelodeon's *Victorious* as a teenager. Artists such as Mariah Carey inspired her to master singing. Her 2013 album *Yours Truly* debuted at number one.

**Birthday:**
June 26, 1993

**Hometown:**
Boca Raton, Florida

**Types of Music:**
dance-pop, R & B, pop hip-hop

**First Hit Song:**
"The Way"

## WICKEDLY SUCCESSFUL

Grande's 2014 album *My Everything* scored four Top 10 hits. Her 2019 album, *thank u, next,* included her first two number one singles. Grande received an Oscar nomination for *Wicked* in 2025.

# HIT RELEASES

***My Everything***
**(2014)**

***Dangerous Woman***
**(2016)**

***Sweetener***
**(2018)**

***thank u, next***
**(2019)**

***eternal sunshine***
**(2024)**

## STREAMING SUPERSTAR

Grande has more than 20 songs with one billion Spotify streams. She has had seven songs debut at number one.

# TIMELINE

**2010**
**Grande stars in Nickelodeon's series *Victorious***

**2013**
**Grande's first album, *Yours Truly*, debuts at number one**

**2019**
***thank u, next* is released and includes Grande's first two number one singles**

**2024**
**"we can't be friends (wait for your love)" becomes Grande's ninth number one single**

**2025**
**Grande receives an Oscar nomination for her role in *Wicked***

# BTS

BTS helped make K-pop popular worldwide. They are one of music's most successful boy bands.

## TRAINING FOR GREATNESS

BTS formed in 2010. The band's members lived and trained together for years. Their first full-length album, *Dark & Wild*, came out in 2014.

## A NUMBER OF FIRSTS

BTS's 2018 album *Love Yourself: Tear* was the first K-pop album to top the *Billboard* 200. Their 2021 song "Butter" scored a record-breaking 108.2 million YouTube views in one day.

## TIMELINE

**2010**
BTS form and begin to train

**2014**
BTS's first full-length album, *Dark & Wild*, debuts

**2018**
*Love Yourself: Tear* is the first K-pop album to top the *Billboard* 200

## K-POP ICONS

BTS are history's best-selling K-pop group. As of 2025, they have topped the *Billboard* Hot 100 six times.

## HIT RELEASES

***Dark & Wild***
**(2014)**

***Wings***
**(2016)**

***Love Yourself: Tear***
**(2018)**

***Map of the Soul: 7***
**(2020)**

***BE***
**(2020)**

**Notable Members:**
Jin, Suga, J-Hope, RM, Jimin, V, Jungkook

**Place Formed:**
Seoul, South Korea

**Dates Active:**
2010–2022;
2025–present

**Types of Music:**
K-pop, R & B, pop rock

**First Hit Song:**
"No More Dream" (2013)

**2020**
BTS become the fastest group since the Beatles to earn four number one albums

**2021**
"Butter" breaks the music video record for most YouTube views in one day

# THE FUTURE OF POP

Pop music continues to change. Technology such as MIDI lets producers create more sounds than ever before. TikTok is also advancing the way pop is made. Many artists now make shorter, simpler songs in hopes of going viral.

BAD BUNNY

Sabrina Carpenter and Tate McRae rule modern streaming charts. Billie Eilish, Olivia Rodrigo, and Chappell Roan bring more alternative sounds to mainstream pop. Bad Bunny and BLACKPINK are helping Latin pop and K-pop grow globally. As the pop genre changes, it keeps fans everywhere singing and dancing!

# GLOSSARY

**acoustic**—sounds or instruments created without the help of electronics

**advocacy**—the act of speaking out and supporting a cause

**airplay**—the amount of times a song is streamed or played on the radio

**alternative**—related to something different and typically outside of the mainstream

**choreography**—a series of dance movements, often by a group

**collaborated**—worked with others to create something

**cultural**—relating to the beliefs, arts, and ways of life in a place or society

**debut**—first appearance

**duo**—a group of two

**Emmy**—a yearly award presented for achievements in TV

**generations**—groups of people who were born around the same time

**genre**—a category for a type of music

**inducted**—to be officially admitted as a member of an organization

**inspired**—gave someone an idea about what to do or create

**LGBTQ+**—a community of people who identify as something other than heterosexual or the gender they were assigned at birth; LGBTQ+ stands for Lesbian, Gay, Bisexual, Transgender, Queer and other identities.

**mainstream**—common and shared by a large audience

**melodies**—series of lyrics and sounds that are arranged with a rhythm

**MIDI**—a tool that allows electric instruments and computers to communicate with one another; MIDI stands for Musical Instrument Digital Interface.

**nomination**—the process of being chosen as a candidate for an award

**Oscar**—a yearly award presented for achievements in film; Oscars are also called Academy Awards.

**rhythms**—strong, regular, repeated patterns of movement or sound

**scholarships**—money to support a student's education

**subgenres**—smaller, more specific types of music within a genre

**synthesizers**—electronic musical instruments that can create sounds and change existing sounds

**viral**—popular from being shared quickly

# WRITE ABOUT IT!

- Which artist do you think has had the biggest impact on pop? **Why?**
- What are some of your favorite pop songs? **Why do you like them?**
- How do you think pop music will continue to **change** in the future?

ALSO CHECK OUT

# INDEX




The images in this book are reproduced through the courtesy of: Gorodenkoff, front cover (hero), p. 4 (left), 5 (top left); Onradio, front cover (bass); brandingfreedom, front cover (speaker); South_agency, fro cover (keyboard singer); Brian Friedman, pp. 3 (Lady Gaga), 34 (botto left), 36 (Lady Gaga), 37 (middle); Featureflash Photo Agency, pp. 3 (Taylor Swift), 34-35 (Taylor Swift), 38 (top right); Northfoto, pp. 3 (Prince), 26-27 (Prince); Christopher Polk/ staff/ Getty Images, p. 4 (Taylor Swift); ZUMA Press, Inc./ Alamy Stock Photo, pp. 4-5; Kevi Mazur/ Contributor/ Getty Images, pp. 5 (top right), 18-19, 29 (top), 43 (top); Bettmann/ Contributor/ Getty Images, p. 6 (left); Throast/ Wikimedia Commons, p. 6 (bottom); David Redfern/ Staff/ Getty Image pp. 6-7; Mary Mead Maddick/ Wikimedia Commons, p. 7 (top); antonmatveev, p. 7 (bottom); Logopedia Wiki/ Wikimedia Commons, pp. 8 (top left), 10 (middle top); Evan Agostini/ AP Images, p. 8 (top right); KMazur/ Contributor/ Getty Images, pp. 8 (middle), 9, 25 (middle); picsmart, p. 8 (bottom); Dave Hogan/ Contributor/ Getty Images, pp. 8-9, 31 (top left, bottom); DANIEL CONSTANTE, p. 9 (mid top); Geoffrey Clowes, p. 9 (middle bottom); The Library of Congress/ Wikimedia Commons, p. 10 (left); Billboard/ Wikimedia Commons, p. 1 (middle); Monkees.com/ Wikimedia Commons, p. 10 (middle bottom); Ron Galella/ Contributor/ Getty Images, pp. 10-11; The_Pixel, p. 11 (top); Ron Galella, Ltd./ Contributor/ Getty Images, pp. 11 (middle left), 15 (top middle); Eugene Powers, p. 11 (middle right); McSleep, p. 11 (bottom); Science & Society Picture Library/ Contributor/ Getty Images, p. 12 (top); Jack Robinson/ Contributor/ Getty Images, p. 12 (middle); Cummings Archives/ Contributor/ Getty Images, p. 12 (bottom); DC Studio, p. 13 (top left); Kevork Djansezian/ Stringer/ Getty Images, p. 13 (top right); Eric Robert/ Contributor/ Getty Images, p. 13 (bottom) Bernd Schwabe/ Wikimedia Commons, pp. 14 (Grammy), 20 (Grammy 29 (Grammy), 32 (Grammy), 35 (Grammy); Ed Widdis/ AP Images, p. 14 (bottom); AFP/ Stringer/ Getty Images, p. 15 (top left); Kathy Hutchins, pp. 15 (Billboard award), 21 (Billboard award), 25 (Billboar award), 27 (Billboard award), 35 (middle), 36 (top), 40 (top left); WFDJ_Stock, pp. 15 (MTV Video Music Award), 33 (MTV Video Music Award); G.PAUL BURNETT/ AP Images, p. 15 (bottom right); GABRIEL DUVAL/ Contributor/ Getty Images, p. 16 (left); BruceC007/ Wikimedi Commons, p. 16 (right); OSCAR GONZALEZ FUENTES, p. 17 (left); Michael Ochs Archives/ Stringer/ Getty Images, pp. 17 (right), 24 (bottom); A.RICARDO, p. 18 (left); Mike Lawrie/ Contributor/ Getty Images, p. 19 (top); Kevin Winter/ Staff/ Getty Images, p. 19 (bottom); ABC Television/ Wikimedia Commons, p. 20 (top left); Casablanca Records/ Wikimedia Commons, p. 20 (top right); Ben Houdijk, pp. 20 (middle left), 45 (middle right, bottom right); Jacob Boomsma, p. 20 (middle); Raph_PH/ Wikimedia Commons, pp. 20 (middle right), 22 (top right); Evgeniy Skripnichenko, pp. 20 (Oscar), 37 (Oscar), 41 (Oscar); Debby Wong, pp. 21 (top), 39 (top); Heritage Auctions/ Wikimedia Commons, p. 21 (midle); Bert Verhoeff for Anefo/ Wikimedia Commons, p. 22 (top left); Paul Natkin/ Contributor/ Getty Images, pp 22 (middle), 25 (top left); Denis Makarenko, p. 22 (bottom left); Nigel Cox/ Wikimedia Commons, p. 22 (bottom right); anyamuse, pp. 22-23; Jørund Føreland Pedersen/ Wikimedia Commons p. 23 (bottom); Cultura Creative, p. 23 (1976); Iranzinrlk/ Wikimedia Commons, p. 24 (top); Matthew Rolston; Distributed by Epic Records/ Wikimedia Commons, p. 24 (middle); Matt Gush, p. 25 (top right); Damian Strohmeyer/ Contributor/ Getty Images, p. 25 (bottom); Jonath Daniel/ Staff/ Getty Images, p. 26 (bottom left); andreykr, p. 26 (botton right); Icon and Image/ Contributor/ Getty Images, p. 27 (top, middle right); Khairil Azhar Junos, p. 27 (middle left); Allen Beaulieu; Distributed by Warner Bros. Records./ Wikimedia Commons, p. 27 (bottom); Micha Putland/ Contributor/ Getty Images, p. 28 (top); picture alliance/ Contributor/ Getty Images, pp. 28 (middle), 30 (bottom left); yakub88, p. 28 (bottom); A.PAES, pp. 29 (middle), 39 (bottom right); nicolemfelte p. 29 (bottom); David Buchan/ Contributor/ Getty Images, pp. 30-31; James Devaney/ Contributor/ Getty Images, p. 30 (middle); Z28scrambler/ Wikimedia Commons, p. 30 (bottom right); Dyllan/ Wikimedia Commons, p. 31 (top right); Glenn Francis/ Wikimedia Commons, p. 31 (middle); Avis De Miranda, pp. 32 (top left) 33 (top); lev radin, pp. 32 (top right), 40 (top right); Andres.Arranz/ Wikimedia Commons, p. 32 (bottom); Roman, p. 33 (middle left); Gusta Miguel Fernandes, p. 33 (middle right); a katz, p. 34 (top left); Paolo Villanueva/ Wikimedia Commons, p. 34 (top right); Brian Cantoni/ Wikimedia Commons, p. 34 (middle left); s_bukley, pp. 34 (middle right 37 (top right); Nimbesi/ Wikimedia Commons, p. 34 (bottom right); Matteo Chinellato, p. 37 (top left); Tierney, p. 37 (bottom); Tinseltown, p. 38 (top left); Jack Fordyce, p. 38 (bottom left); JHVEPhoto, p. 38 (bottom right); Variety/ Contributor/ Getty Images, p. 39 (bottom left); Alexander Tamargo/ Contributor/ Getty Images, p. 40 (middle left Jin, p. 40 (middle right); FashionStock.com, p. 40 (bottom left); Frazer Harrison/ Staff/ Getty Images, p. 40 (bottom right); ROBYN BECK/ Contributor/ Getty Images, p. 41; Han Myung-Gu/ Contributor/ Getty Images, p. 42 (top); Silvia Elizabeth Pangaro, p. 42 (middle); Chris Pizzello/ AP Images, p. 42 (bottom); POOJA SAINI, p. 43 (middle left); Toowongsa, p. 43 (middle right); Best smile studio, p. 44 (top); Eduardo Manurae, p. 44 (middle); Sudarsan Thobias, p. 44 (bottom); Kristy Sparow/ Contributor/ Getty Images, p. 45 (top); lev radin, p. 45 (middle left); L Paul Mann, p. 45 (bottom left).